# THE MIRACLE MAKER

## The greatest story ever told

Sally Humble-Jackson

*Hodder
Children's
Books*

a division of Hodder Headline Ltd

# Chapter 1

I'm all right!' grumbled Tamar, as her father gripped her hand. Honestly, she wasn't a baby!

But to Jairus, Tamar still felt like his baby. Her skin was so smooth, her curls as soft as a new-born lamb's. Tears stung his eyes.

'Really, Father!' Tamar wriggled her fingers. 'I'm all right.'

Jairus sighed. If she were really all right, they wouldn't be here now, pushing their way through these dreadful crowds, searching for the doctor's house.

His heart ached. Why was God making his child suffer? He knew God's reasons are always good, but right now, climbing the steps to the doctor's rooms, it was hard to understand.

Tamar waited outside, fascinated by the city. There was so much to see - builders building, a carpenter hammering, a strange woman lurching along the street. Tamar could tell straight away that the woman was mad. She thought all the men were in love with her - but they weren't. In fact, the builders were all horrible to her.

Except the carpenter... He looked at the woman and frowned. He put down his tools.

Tamar was so busy watching that she didn't hear the doctor's serious voice, nor the choked noise her father made. She didn't hear the doctor saying that she would get worse... that there was no cure. But she heard the dull thud as one of the builders knocked the mad woman to the ground, heard the poor soul cry out in pain and fear.

The carpenter heard it too. He took a deep breath, left his work, and knelt beside the poor creature. Gently he lifted her from the dust.

Jairus also took a deep breath. He stepped out into the sunshine, struggling to hide his despair from Tamar.

'Father, look!'

Jairus glanced around. A drunken woman - right in front of the synagogue - the holy place of God! He must have been mad to expect a miracle in a place like this!

'Come away!' he called, and Tamar followed. She had no choice.

As they left the city, Tamar gazed back at the carpenter. He'd been so kind, not angry at all. And that, somehow, had made the other men feel ashamed.

The carpenter caught her glance - and his heart stood still. Who would have guessed that this beloved child needed him; needed him every bit as badly as the lonely mad woman. Until now, only God had known such things. But if God, his Father in Heaven, knew it, from now on Jesus would know it, too.

Slowly the carpenter walked away from the city. His Father was calling him, louder and louder, and he had to follow. He had no choice.

# Chapter 2

As Jesus walked home to Nazareth, he wondered how his mother had felt when God had called her. Would she have chosen to give birth in a stable? To have shown her baby to wise men and shepherds? Had she found it easy to obey?

But if Jesus thought he had no choice, he soon discovered he was wrong. Not because God's call faded - in fact, when Jesus went to the river to be baptised, it was so loud that others heard it too. But because another voice called him, too - the voice of the devil. 'Choose...' it urged. 'Choose to disobey.'

For six long weeks Jesus wandered the bare mountains, listening to that other voice. The sun beat down, the streams dried up, the parched leaves rattled in the spiteful wind.

'Choose my way...' whispered the voice.

'No!' blazed Jesus at last. No! He chose God's way - and suddenly it was easy to choose, easy to obey. He wanted to do his Father's work, wanted it more than anything in the world. And the moment he chose, he was filled with such power and such love that the other voice flew away on the spiteful wind.

He tried to explain his new life to his friends, as he sat

with them, sharing their meal.

'But you're a carpenter, building a synagogue...' protested Lazarus.

'Not any more. I'm building something new now. God's kingdom... on earth, as it is in heaven.'

'God's kingdom?' echoed Lazarus' sister Mary, with a frown.

At that moment Martha, the elder sister, approached with a tray of food.

'Jesus,' she grumbled, 'don't you care that my sister has left me to do everything? Tell her to help me!'

But Jesus just laughed and took Martha's hand. 'You do so much for everyone else,' he said tenderly, 'but don't miss the one thing that matters for you. Sit with us. Listen.'

Martha was about to argue that getting the food on the table was the most important thing, when she glanced at her brother and sister. Whatever Jesus had been saying had made them excited, eager, full of wonder. She could see it in their eyes. She sat down and started to listen. Before long her eyes were shining too, as she heard of the kingdom, waiting for Jesus to build it.

# Chapter 3

Everywhere Jesus went he found people hungry for a new kingdom. For two thousand years the Jews had lived by God's laws - but now the Romans made them obey Caesar's laws as well. Had God forgotten them?

'No!' Jesus told them. 'Your Father in heaven longs to give you good gifts! Just ask - and it will be given to you.'

'Our Father?' A work-hardened fisherman imagined loving arms wrapping around him. Andrew had never heard God described like that. He leant forward to hear what this new teacher would say next.

'Seek and you will find,' Jesus promised. 'Knock, and the door will be opened.'

The priests and teachers of God's laws - Sadducees and Pharisees - also listened carefully. Some found their hearts stirred, but others were worried. Such a different way of teaching... and so many people wanting to listen...

The people certainly worried Tamar's mother. Rachel needed to get her daughter home, but they couldn't get past.

'Come to me!' Jesus' voice was so clear, so powerful, that it carried over the crowd. 'And listen!'

'It's him!' Tamar grabbed her mother's sleeve excitedly. 'The carpenter in Sepphoris!'

'And ACT on my words!' Jesus commanded.

Tamar's mother stood still.

'If you do that, you're like a very wise man who built his house on a rock...'

A story! Tamar beamed as she settled down to listen. And this was a great story, about two men. One worked hard and built his house on rock. The other was lazy and built a house on sand, which was much quicker and easier. When there was a storm, the house on the rock was safe, but the house built on sand fell down. All the children laughed. But then the carpenter said something which made everyone stop laughing. He said that some people built their lives the easy way, on sand. When things went wrong, their lives fell to pieces.

'Take the hard way,' said Jesus. 'Let my words go deeper and deeper.'

Rachel nodded, thoughtfully - then she glanced at Tamar. Oh no, too much sun...

'Let me stay,' pleaded Tamar.

'Come to me,' said Jesus. 'Everyone who is hungry...'

Tamar's knees buckled.

'I will never, ever turn away,' Jesus promised.

But Rachel had already turned away, carrying Tamar in her arms. Her fever was back.


Someone else walked away from Jesus that day, to fetch his comrades to listen.

'No!' roared their leader, Bar-Abbas.

'The people love him,' Judas protested. 'They say that he has powers... from God.'

Bar-Abbas sneered. 'What power can one man have against the might of Caesar!'

Judas gripped his friend's shoulder.

'What do kings and emperors fear?' he demanded. 'They fear the people, when they follow ONE MAN!'

For a moment Bar-Abbas hesitated. Long ago, God had promised to send one man to save them - the Messiah. Had Judas found the Messiah, the one who would lead them into battle against Rome?

No! How could a teacher from a tiny village like Nazareth be the Messiah?

'Dreams,' Bar-Abbas muttered scornfully.

So Judas walked away - back to Jesus.

# Chapter 4

It wasn't hard to find him. Wherever he went, people followed. Not the rich - who liked their easy lives - but the rest. They had nothing to lose: they'd already lost it to the tax-collectors. The tax-collectors had once been ordinary Jews, until the Romans gave them a job. Now they were seen as scum, who took money from their own people - and kept half for themselves.

They even tried to take taxes from the poor mad woman, Mary Magdalene.

'Thieves! Murderers!' she shrieked, throwing her few miserable coins on the ground.

'Leave her be,' muttered one of the guards.

Matthew, the tax collector, sighed. She'd crossed the border so she had to pay. It wasn't his fault - he didn't make the rules.

'How much does she owe?'

'Nothing!' spat an angry fisherman, glaring at Matthew. 'And nor do we. We caught nothing. No catch, no money.'

Matthew flinched. Was he to blame if the nets came up empty? 'It's the law,' he tried to explain, over the din of the mad woman, who was screeching some nonsense about the Emperor.

'Is it the law for you to cheat?' snarled the fisherman -

but before he could say more, his brother grabbed him.

'Simon!' gasped Andrew. 'He's here! The man I told you about! He's coming down to the shore.'

'So?'

'He's the one God has sent to save us.'

Simon shrugged as he strode back to his boat. He ignored Jesus, and the crowd following him.

'Tie up the boats and don't pay,' Simon muttered to James and John, who were also fishermen.

Jesus watched them for a moment, then he stepped into Simon and Andrew's boat. He tried not to laugh at Simon's shocked expression.

'Push the boat out!'

'What?'

'Do you want everyone else to come on board, too?'

Simon scowled as he nudged the boat out from the crowded dock.

'What is the Kingdom of Heaven like?' Jesus began, studying the eager faces on the shore. He caught Matthew's eye. The tax-collector's heart missed a beat. No-one ever met his eye.

'I'll tell you. It's like... a mustard seed. It's so small, it could blow away. And yet it becomes the greatest tree of all! And all the birds come and make their nests in its branches.'

Simon frowned. So the Kingdom of Heaven grows from nothing, into a home... a shelter?

Matthew looked uneasily at the flimsy roof of his tax-booth. One day an angry fisherman was going to knock it to the ground. He imagined himself flying to the safety of a tree, high in the branches where nothing could hurt him. And then he closed his eyes and sighed. Who'd want him in their tree? No-one.

The boat drifted. The sun beat down. Jesus looked out over the sparkling water to the tax-booth, to Matthew. Even from so far away Jesus could see the glitter of tears. He trailed his fingers in the cool water, watching Simon wrestling with his anger, Andrew beaming with simple pleasure, James and John in their boat, lost in thought.

'Push the boat further out.' Jesus smiled at the fishermen. 'Let down your nets for a catch.'

Simon growled with disgust. Didn't the man know anything? You couldn't catch fish in the middle of the day - they hid from the sunlight, right down in the depths.

He only lowered the nets so that Jesus could see for himself. But what Jesus did see - and Simon and Andrew, too - was fish. The water was empty but the nets were full to bursting!

As Simon brought the miraculous catch ashore, he groaned with shame. Why did he always think he knew best? What was the matter with him? Fancy thinking he knew better than a messenger of God...

'Simon, don't be afraid,' Jesus said gently. 'From today, I'm going to make you a fisher of men! I shall call you

Peter - the Rock.'

Simon was startled. A rock? Was Jesus joking?

But Jesus seemed perfectly serious as he chose the men who would one day take God's message to the world.

'Andrew, you'll be my apostle, too,' he announced. 'And James and John.'

The four fishermen beamed with pleasure. So did Philip and Bartholomew, James and Simon, Thaddeus and Thomas - though it took Thomas a few moments to believe that Jesus really wanted him! Judas glowed with pride when he was chosen.

'One more,' said Jesus, making his way to the tax-booth.

But Simon-Peter knew better. 'Master, this is not a good place,' he warned.

Matthew kept his head bowed. How he wished he had never become a tax-collector. Then he might have been able to look Jesus in the eye.

'Matthew!' Jesus' voice was strong and clear.

Matthew began to shake. More insults... more anger.... 'Matthew,' called Jesus again, 'follow me!'

Baffled, Matthew lifted his head. He looked Jesus in the eye. And what he saw there filled his heart with longing. All the things he'd done wrong... they didn't matter any more. His sins had been forgiven! Slowly he got to his feet. With trembling hands he threw down his money and went to Jesus' side.

Matthew? The tax-collector? The others were shocked - but when they saw the love in Jesus' eyes, they felt ashamed of themselves.

# Chapter 5

The twelve apostles followed Jesus everywhere. It was wonderful, watching him use his Father's power to cure the sick, to call the needy. All who came to him were healed by his touch, helped by his teachings.

Simon-Peter loved fishing for people - though, of course, there were some who refused to listen, like fish hiding from the sunlight.

Ben Azra, for instance, had grown rich and powerful by helping the Romans keep the peace. He thought people would tire of this magician from Nazareth, but as the months passed, the crowds just got bigger. He brought his friends to see the danger. Some could see only good, but some could see the danger, too.

Simon-Peter could see plenty of danger that day. Jesus was teaching in Simon-Peter's house - and it was jam-packed! He was telling a story about a man who thought he knew better than everyone else. Simon-Peter pictured the man with a log in his eye, yet certain that he could see dust in other people's eyes, and he winced. Was he like that? But before he could decide, he really did get dust in his eyes.

'What's going on?' Simon-Peter bellowed. Oh no! Some men were tearing open his roof to get their sick friend to Jesus.

Jesus looked up.

'Come on down,' he laughed. 'There's plenty of room.'

Plenty of room? Simon-Peter almost exploded.

Gently the man was lowered through the roof, lying on a thin mattress.

'It's no good,' groaned the man, as Jesus helped him down. He hadn't been able to move a muscle for years. 'Just let me die...'

Jesus touched his forehead. 'My friend,' he murmured, but the man screwed up his face, as if he didn't deserve friendship.

'My friend,' said Jesus firmly, 'your sins are forgiven.'

Ben Azra sneered. Who can forgive sins but God?

Jesus looked into Ben Azra's eyes. 'Which is it easier to say,' he demanded, 'your sins are forgiven? Or - get up and walk? But to prove to you that the Son of Man has the power to forgive sins...' He turned back to the sick man, 'Pick up your bed. And walk!'

The sick man blinked. He sat up. Then he got to his feet, picked up his mattress and let out a cry of joy! Roars of delight followed him as he ran through the streets.

'I'm healed!' he cried.

Jairus saw the man and sighed. This wasn't right... God had his reasons for letting people suffer. No man should meddle with God's will.

'I'm healed!'

Rachel saw the man. She looked at Tamar, so pale and

weak, and her heart stirred.

'I'm healed!'

Tamar saw the man, too, and she knew that he had been touched by Jesus. What else could fill someone with such joy?

But Mary Magdalene wasn't filled with joy. All she ever felt was terror and rage. Her head was crowded with voices, horrible voices.

Sometimes they sneered. Sometimes they bellowed and blared and cackled and screeched and taunted and tormented. She stumbled blindly, feeling as if her head would burst.

Jesus' face was a blur. Jesus' hand was no more than the brush of a bat-wing in the dark. He was just another stranger.

But the voices in her head knew him. They shrieked with terror.

'Come out of her!' he charged.

The voices panicked. 'We know who you are - Jesus, Son of God!'

'Let her go!' Jesus roared.

The voices fled, streaming away on the wind. Glorious silence filled Mary Magdalene's head. She looked at Jesus, and the eyes which met hers were no longer the eyes of a stranger.

From then on Mary Magdalene stayed with the

women who followed Jesus. She let his words go deeper and deeper, as he taught. At last she knew the meaning of peace.

Rachel couldn't find peace. Her child was sick, and growing worse as the months went by. She yearned to take Tamar to Jesus - but Jairus refused.

'Please...' she begged Cleopas, their oldest friend, 'tell him.'

Cleopas bit his lip. 'How is she?'

'She's dying!' Rachel admitted bitterly.

'No!' protested Jairus. 'She is not dying!'

Rachel clenched her fists. Why was her husband so stubborn? He and his friends - all priests and teachers of God's laws - they talked about God, but they wouldn't listen!

'Are you so afraid of your friends?' she accused her husband. 'Have they got such a hold over your life?'

'God is my life,' snapped Jairus. 'Not any man!'

Rachel breathed deeply. 'And your daughter,' she asked coldly, 'what is she, in your life?'

Jairus was stunned. Rachel had never spoken like this before.

It was Cleopas who broke the silence. 'I think we should listen to this Jesus,' he said thoughtfully. 'After all, no-one ever lost their soul by listening to a liar. Only by believing him and following.'

Simon the Pharisee gasped. Was Cleopas mad? Surely they all agreed that Jesus' powers came from the devil...?

'You must listen,' Rachel urged.

'Why should people think their leaders do not listen?' muttered the powerful Pharisee uneasily.

So Simon the Pharisee invited Jesus and his disciples to a banquet. The Pharisee's rich friends stared at the work-hardened fishermen with Jesus, and exchanged uneasy glances. Jairus shook his head. What was the point of this?

'We know you would rather be eating with tax-collectors and sinners,' sighed one of the Pharisee's friends. 'Why is that?'

'Those who are well don't need a doctor,' Jesus explained carefully, as if these wealthy men were slightly stupid, 'only those who are sick.'

The guests frowned. They were struggling to think of some better questions - ones which Jesus couldn't answer so cleverly - when a woman pushed past the servants and fell at Jesus' feet.

Mary Magdalene burst into tears - all those servants chasing her, treating her as if she were still mad. When she remembered the terrible life she had lived as an outcast, she just wanted to keep thanking Jesus. As her tears dripped on his feet, she dried them with her hair.

'She's a sinner!' shuddered Simon the Pharisee.

But Jesus shook his head. 'All your sins have been forgiven now, Mary,' he reminded her.

'Saying he can forgive sins... Only God can forgive sins,' the guests hissed. 'Now we know for sure. Anyone following Jesus is an enemy of God.'

Slowly Jairus nodded his head.

# Chapter 6

Jesus never stopped being glad that he'd chosen his Father's way - even though it was sometimes puzzling. The child, Tamar, for instance... He longed to go to her. But his Father in Heaven knew better. Jesus must wait. People must come to him... That was the choice that they must make.

But Tamar had no choice. The fever and the pain grew so bad that she couldn't even leave her bed. Rachel and Jairus felt their hearts breaking.

'Father...' Tamar whispered, 'am I going to die?'

Jairus felt his mouth dry up. 'No...'

Rachel touched her husband's arm. 'She keeps saying his name - Jesus.'

'No!' Jairus said loudly.

Rachel's eyes filled with tears.

Jairus shook his head. No! He wouldn't listen to anyone else any longer... He'd seen Jesus, heard Jesus. Such love... such goodness... it had to come from God.

'I will go to Jesus,' he promised.

Tamar struggled to open her clouded eyes. Jairus saw a glimmer of joy there, but he also saw something else - death. She was slipping away...

He ran - the man who taught God's laws ran through the streets like a desperate criminal.

The people around Jesus had walked for days to hear him, but there was something in Jairus' face that made the crowds part for him.

The moment Jairus looked into Jesus' eyes he began to cry. He fell to the ground, crippled by shame. This man had been sent by God... and he had been such a fool... he didn't deserve help.

'My little girl,' Jairus begged, 'she's dying. Please - if you come now and lay your hands on her, she will be healed.'

When Jesus nodded, Jairus felt his heart would burst. How good God was! He stumbled to his feet and began to lead the way. But they hadn't gone far when Jesus stopped.

'Hurry,' Jairus breathed. 'Please hurry!'

'Who touched me?' Jesus asked, bewildered. 'Someone did. I felt the power go out of me.'

Simon-Peter pulled a face. Hundreds of people had touched him! Only one person understood what Jesus meant. A woman had touched his robe, and had felt his power enter her.

'It... was me, master,' she confessed. 'I... was bleeding inside for so many years...' She wrung her hands. 'I was afraid to come to you before all the people so... so...'

Jairus held his breath. All he could see were Tamar's eyes, dark and cloudy...

'Your faith has made you well,' Jesus said, and he said it with such love that the woman's face filled with joy. But Jairus saw nothing of it. His eyes were fixed on the faces of two of his own servants, walking gravely towards him, their heads bowed.

Tamar had died. It was too late.

Jairus began to weep. He had been wrong... And now his beloved child had paid the price for his doubts.

Jesus came to comfort him. 'Keep on believing,' he said urgently, 'and she will be well.'

Jairus studied Jesus' face. Yes... he would keep on believing... but he didn't understand...

Jesus entered Jairus' house and went straight to the dead child. He touched Tamar's cold, lifeless hand.

'Little girl,' he said with a smile in his voice, 'it's time to get up.'

Jairus and Rachel watched, bewildered. Tamar was dead. How could she get up? Simon-Peter shook his head; this was impossible! Only Tamar was neither puzzled nor confused. She yawned and stretched and opened her eyes - and when she saw Jesus she flung herself into his arms.

'You came!' she cried. 'You came!'

'Yes, I'm here,' Jesus laughed. He turned to her parents. 'She's hungry,' he teased, 'get her something to eat'.

But Tamar had no time for food. At last - at long last - she really was all right! She danced around the room and ran outside, laughing and shouting... and everyone who saw her was filled to the brim with joy.

'Ask and it shall be given to you,' Jesus had promised.

'Seek, and you will find.'

Jairus had asked - now he began to seek. He followed Jesus everywhere - and so did Tamar and Rachel and Cleopas.

As the months passed, they watched Jesus healing and teaching, eating and drinking, laughing and praying - but always, always building God's kingdom.

Even so, Jairus found some things hard to understand. If God was a loving father, how could he be a law-giver too?

Tamar laughed. Her father often said that he was only strict because he loved her. Wasn't that the same thing?

'It's easy,' she explained. 'There are two really important laws now - love God with all your heart, and love other people, even if they're hard to love. That's what Jesus says!'

# Chapter 7

For three years, Jesus had been teaching that God's kingdom was coming. As they travelled to Jerusalem for the Passover feast, Jesus told his disciples that God's kingdom would come soon. Judas was thrilled. Jerusalem was the heart of the Jewish faith - and the home of the Roman government. Judas knew this was where the battle had to be fought if there were to be no more Roman laws, only God's law.

Jews were pouring into Jerusalem. Pilate, the Roman governor, was used to it - but he didn't like it.

'This Passover...' he explained to his new army officer, 'it's a festival of freedom. Something about Egyptians... some old story.'

Pilate shivered secretly at the thought of the old story, about a leader called Moses, who once led the Jews against the mighty Egyptians - and won. Leaders could still cause trouble.

'I hear,' Pilate continued, 'you've already put down a Jewish revolt in Galilee?'

'A hundred and seventeen crucified, sir!'

'And the leaders?'

'Bar-Abbas and his friends -'

'Ah yes,' smiled Pilate. 'They're the ones to be executed in Jerusalem on the day of the Passover.' That would teach the

Jews a lesson they wouldn't forget!

It was a long journey to Jerusalem. Jesus and his disciples camped in fields beside the road. Waking at dawn with the mist still thick on the ground, Tamar had never been so happy in all her life.

The disciples were excited at the idea of the new kingdom. As they gathered round fires in the evening they wondered which of them would be in charge.

Jesus picked up a tiny child. 'Unless you change,' he warned his disciples, 'and become like little children, you will never even enter the Kingdom of Heaven.'

The disciples were puzzled - but Tamar wasn't. The grown-ups always thought they knew best - but children understood that Jesus knew best.

'What must we do to be saved?' asked a worried teacher of the law.

Jesus said, 'You must trust God with all your heart and love your neighbour as much as you love yourself.'

'And... and who is my neighbour?'

Tamar smiled. She knew what would happen next: Jesus would tell one of his stories. Would this teacher of the law and all the grown-ups listen to the story as if they were children?

For once they did. It was a creepy story, about a man who was travelling along a lonely road when he was beaten up by robbers.

They left him at the side of the road. A priest came along, but didn't want to touch a dead person, so he hurried past in case the man was dead. And then a rich teacher of the law came along, and he hurried by too. Then along came a man from Samaria.

The children listening all jeered. Nobody liked the Samaritans. But when Jesus frowned they remembered guiltily that God wanted them to love their enemies. Anyway, this Samaritan was sorry for the poor man and he bandaged his wounds and took him to an inn and paid the inn-keeper to look after him and make him better.

'Now,' said Jesus, staring at the grown-ups, 'which of these three men proved to be the man's neighbour?'

'The one who showed him such love,' stammered the teacher of the law, feeling ashamed of himself.

'Well,' said Jesus, 'then you go and do the same.'

# Chapter 8

A s they approached Jerusalem, a vast crowd gathered, thousands upon thousands, all waving palm branches and crying out to Jesus, calling him King. But instead of sweeping grandly into the city, he chose to ride on a tiny donkey. Judas didn't understand - but Tamar did. He was the prince of peace. How else should he come?

Ben Azra hurried to the temple to warn the chief priest about the crowd. 'They'll follow him anywhere... to war... We'll have to stop him.'

Caiaphas narrowed his eyes. Jesus must die. But for that to happen, Jesus must be shown to break the law - Roman law.

Jesus went straight to the courtyard of the great temple. He remembered being brought here as a boy, when it had been a peaceful place, full of good priests, discussing God's laws. Now it was a marketplace, full of people trading in God's holy place.

Suddenly Jesus was filled with rage. He swept the money-changers' tables to the ground. 'My Father's house,' he roared, 'is a house of prayer, but you have turned it into a den of thieves!'

Ben Azra nudged a man forward. This was the perfect time to trick Jesus - when he was angry. The man called out, 'Master, is it right for us to pay taxes to Caesar?' When

Jesus answered 'No!' they'd arrest him.

But Jesus didn't say 'No'. Instead he asked the man to hold up a Roman coin. It showed Caesar's head.

'You give to Caesar what belongs to Caesar,' he commanded. 'But give to God what belongs to God.'

Ben Azra groaned.

Judas groaned, too. Telling people to pay taxes to Rome... This was no way to start a war against the Romans!

Later, when Jesus warned his disciples that soon he would die, Judas turned away in despair. Had he wasted three years, following a leader who wanted to die? As he walked away he passed the Roman dungeons. Through iron bars he glimpsed Bar-Abbas and his friends from Galilee, bound and chained. For a moment he thought he would faint. The ground beneath him didn't seem solid, it felt like wet sand. Was there no-one left to stand up to the Romans? No-one at all? He marched straight to Ben Azra and offered to help capture Jesus.

Jesus spent his days teaching in the courtyard of the temple. He spent the nights on the Mount of Olives, where many people camped during Passover. The priests didn't want to start a riot by arresting Jesus in front of a crowd, but sooner or later Jesus must go off alone to pray... and when he did, Judas would tell them.

At sunset, on the eve of the Passover, every Jew in the

world shared a meal with his family and friends. Jesus borrowed a large upstairs room in Jerusalem for his most loyal followers. There would be no huge crowd that night.

Tamar was puzzled as they gathered for the meal. 'Why are we meeting in secret?'

'Because Jesus is safer here,' Mary Magdalene explained.

'No-one will arrest him at Passover,' Cleopas reassured her.

Tamar gasped. Arrest him? Why would anyone want to arrest him?

Jesus thanked God for the bread, holding it high as he always did. Then Jesus broke the bread and handed it to his disciples. 'Take and eat,' he said lovingly. 'This is my body, which is broken for you.'

The disciples exchanged puzzled glances. Tamar bit her lip.

Then he blessed the wine and sipped the dark liquid. 'Drink from this, all of you,' he said, handing the cup on, 'for this is my blood, which is poured out for many, for the forgiveness of sins.'

'No!' cried Simon-Peter angrily.

But Tamar just felt sad. Broken? Bleeding? It must be true, if Jesus said so.

'One of you is going to betray me,' Jesus explained. Surprisingly, he didn't sound angry. He sounded as if he understood.

'No!' Simon Peter's face burned. 'I'll NEVER, let you down! I won't leave you...'

But Jesus was shaking his head. 'Simon-Peter,' he said tenderly, 'by the time the cock crows today you will have denied three times that you know me.'

Tamar felt tears springing to her eyes as she looked at Simon-Peter. He looked so dismayed, so baffled. He loved Jesus so much... And he thought he was ready to die for Jesus. But he wasn't, because he still thought that what he wanted was more important than what God wanted. She sighed. Would she be like that when she grew up?

Then Jesus went to Judas. 'Judas, go and do what you have to do,' he said quietly.

Judas' blood ran cold.

'Go and do it quickly,' Jesus insisted, and Judas did, because - well, if Jesus told him to do it then it must be right...

# Chapter 9

That night Jesus took three of his disciples and left their camp.

Tamar chased after him.

'Where are you going?' she asked anxiously. 'I don't want you to go.'

Jesus stroked her hair.

'Don't be upset,' he said. 'In my father's house there are so many rooms... I'm going to find a wonderful place for you. One day, you'll always be with me.'

Tamar felt tears spill down her cheeks as Jesus walked off into the darkness. One day she would be with him in paradise - but first God wanted him to be broken, like the bread.

Jesus, too, felt tears gathering as he stood alone beneath the stars. For three years he had chosen to do everything his Father's way, to obey his Father in everything. But how could he choose to leave this precious life, this time on earth... the love of his mother, of his friends... of the little children who came to him.

'Father!' he begged, his voice raw. 'Father, let there be some other way! Listen... if there is another way... a way out...'

There was another way - a way out. He didn't have to be broken. All he had to do was listen to the other voice,

Tamar waited, fascinated by the city.

'The Kingdom of Heaven is like a mustard seed,' said Jesus.

'Little girl,' Jesus said, 'it's time to get up.'

Jesus chose to ride into the city on a donkey.

'Give to Caesar what belongs to Caesar,' Jesus commanded.

'I'm washing my hands of this. . .' Pilate cried.

'Father ... I give YOU my spirit.'

'The Kingdom of God has come, and now he is
with us forever,' said Tamar.

the devil's voice which whispered on the spiteful wind, urging him to turn away, to follow the other path, the easy path.

'No!' he roared. 'It's not my will that matters. It's your will, Father. Let your will be done!'

He was ready to face what God chose. His three disciples had fallen asleep. He woke them and waited.

Judas arrived. He kissed Jesus, to show that this was the one.

And then the soldiers appeared, brandishing swords and spears. Simon-Peter tried to fight them off, but Jesus wouldn't let him.

'My Father could send twelve legions of angels to my rescue, if I asked. But that is not the way.'

No... this was the way... being tied and beaten... being pushed and shoved... being treated like a criminal... alone... in the dark... This was his Father's way, and so this must be his way too. And as the ropes cut tighter, the blows grew more savage, he chose it gladly. But it still hurt.

They dragged Jesus to the house of Caiaphas, the chief priest. Ben Azra had summoned some of the priests' Council - but only the ones he could trust to do as he wanted.

Outside, Simon-Peter waited. Would they arrest him next? He covered his head.

Caiaphas glared at Jesus, 'If you are the Messiah, tell

us.'

'You do not believe anything I say,' Jesus pointed out, then added powerfully, 'but soon the Son of Man will be seated beside the throne of God.'

'So you are the Son of God, then?' asked Ben Azra.

Jesus looked steadily back. 'It is you who are saying so.'

Caiaphas shrugged. Clever words - but they'd do him no good. He sent Jesus to the Romans. They had the power to order his death.

Someone recognised Simon-Peter as a follower of Jesus. It was the third time that night.

'You're mad,' he scowled. 'In God's name, I never even met the man!'

In the distance, a cock crowed. Tears filled Simon-Peter's eyes, bitter tears that washed the dust from his eyes, that helped him see himself more clearly. It was then he saw Jesus being led away.

Judas, too, saw Jesus being hauled through the night. He snatched at Ben Azra's robe. 'I've made a mistake!' he cried.

But Ben Azra only smiled.

# Chapter 10

Pilate was furious. He was expected to conduct a trial - in the middle of the night. Really, this was the limit!

'This man is the enemy of Rome,' Caiaphas insisted. 'Jesus... from Galilee.'

Jesus? Pilate frowned. He studied the prisoner curiously. The prisoner looked back, right into his eyes. He was very calm. Most people were frightened of Pilate, of his power - but this man didn't look as if he was afraid of any power on earth.

'Are you... the King of the Jews?' Pilate drawled.

'These are your words,' Jesus said.

And that was all he said. How extraordinary... most prisoners gabbled like parrots, desperate to save their skins. Pilate squirmed. This man was no criminal.

'If he's from Galilee,' Pilate pointed out, 'Herod should try him.'

Herod was frightened of Jesus. The Romans had made Herod King of the Jews. Herod was a Jew and he knew that their true king was the one whom God chose, not the Romans.

This Jesus... what if he was the one? Oh dear - better not to think... better to taunt Jesus... mock him.

They even put a robe and a crown of thorns on him

so that people could see what a shabby sort of king Jesus made. But to Herod's dismay, the crown of thorns made Jesus seem more royal than ever. He found he couldn't order this man's death - not even to please the Romans.

It was barely dawn when Jesus was returned to Pilate. Even so, Ben Azra had drummed up a small crowd.

Pilate was horrified to see him back. 'Don't you realise,' Pilate asked Jesus, ' I have the power to release you or to crucify you?'

'You would have no power over me, if it had not been given to you from above.'

Pilate swallowed hard. 'Who are you?'

But Jesus made no reply.

Panic-stricken, Pilate swung to face the crowd. 'You have a custom - to release one prisoner at Passover,' he pleaded. 'Shall I release the King of the Jews?'

A voice called for Bar-Abbas to be freed... and the rest joined in.

'The murderer?' Pilate said, baffled. 'Don't you want your king?'

'The only king we want is Caesar,' said Caiaphas smoothly.

Pilate could hardly breathe. Every time he dared look at Jesus, Jesus looked back with love and pity in his eyes. Pilate couldn't - wouldn't - be responsible for this man's death. He began to wash his hands, over and over.

'I'm washing my hands of this...' he cried, his voice cracking with emotion.

'Crucify him!' roared the crowd.

'Deal with him according to Roman law,' Pilate muttered, walking away.

Roman law laid a cross as heavy as a tree across Jesus' back and made him drag it through the streets.

His friends camped on the Mount of Olives heard the news. They began to run.

'They're killing him!' roared Jairus, as if his heart was being torn out. Tamar ran at her father's heels as the crowd followed Jesus for the last time.

It was an agony to see him. Bowed beneath the weight, broken and bleeding, he stumbled and fell like a little child.

Tamar touched his hand.

His mother, his disciples, his friends... all the nameless people who had come to him hungry, and had been fed, followed him now to the hill where the scum of the earth were crucified.

Tamar closed her eyes. The cross was raised. The waiting began.

For the two men crucified with Jesus, it was over. But

Jesus could still choose.

'He saved everyone else,' sneered Ben Azra, 'why doesn't he save himself?'

'Come down,' urged the voice of the devil. 'Prove your power.'

Jesus looked down. He saw Tamar. He saw the pain in her heart.

Even children could not understand this... But they would understand... if he followed his Father's way.

A spiteful wind blew in from the desert. Black clouds covered the face of the earth.

'Father!' croaked Jesus with the last of his breath. 'Father... I give YOU my spirit.'

Beneath Tamar's feet the earth shivered, like wet sand.

Tamar helped the women take down the broken body. She remembered Jesus holding the bread high. 'Broken for you...' she remembered. But why? She didn't understand...

They wrapped him in linen cloths.

The Roman Officer trembled. He had crucified so many... but never had he seen a man give up his life as if it were a gift.

A teacher of the law, ashamed of what had been done, gave his own tomb for Jesus.

In their palaces Pilate and Herod sat alone.

Simon-Peter envied the two men who had died at Jesus' side. At last he understood. Better to have stood with him and died with him, than to live without him.

# Chapter 11

The next day was the Sabbath. The loyal friends came together in the room where they had eaten their last meal. Together they rested according to God's law. Together they wept.

But Mary Magdalene couldn't rest. Next day, at dawn after the Sabbath had ended, she visited the tomb. Perhaps there she would find peace.

But there was no peace to be found. Someone had opened the tomb and stolen Jesus' body. She began to cry as if her heart would break. He had gone - and there was no trace of him left...

Someone asked, 'Why are you crying?'

She tried to reply but her tears got in the way.

'Tell me who you're looking for.'

'Oh, Sir, if you're the gardener... please tell me where they've taken him...'

'Mary...'

It was said with love. Mary's skin prickled. In all her life only one person had ever spoken her name like that.

'Jesus?' She blinked away the tears and she saw him. Smiling at her - with love.

She touched him! He was alive! Mary's heart filled to

the brim with joy.

'Go,' he urged. 'Tell everyone. Tell Simon-Peter!'

She ran like a mad-woman back to the city, crying and laughing and screaming out her joy.

'He's alive!' she cried, grabbing Simon-Peter.

'The grief has made you mad.' But the words were no sooner out of Simon-Peter's mouth than he felt ashamed of himself. Why did he think he knew better than Mary? He ran with her, back to the tomb. When he got there he saw Jesus. And Jesus had forgiven him - everything.


Back in the upper room the disciples struggled to understand as Mary and Simon-Peter spilled out their news.

'Everyone's going mad,' Thomas muttered. 'I'm leaving...'

But before he could go, in burst Jairus and Cleopas - and they too were brimful of joy, and struggling to explain.

Jairus told how he'd sent Rachel and Tamar to friends, outside Jerusalem, for safety. Later, he and Cleopas had set off themselves. On the way a man joined them... and as they walked they talked about Jesus. Then the stranger came into the house at Emmaus, and he blessed the bread holding it high above his head, and suddenly they all knew who he was!

At last Tamar understood. Jesus had died to show that

death is not the end.

People didn't always believe that Tamar had really died. But Jesus' death was different. This was a death that no-one could argue with - not priests, not Romans, not anyone. This was the worst kind of death. A public death. Nailed to a cross. Dying in front of everyone's eyes. Dying in front of the whole world.

'Then he was gone!' cried Cleopas, laughing. 'Vanished.'

'No-one there,' said Thomas scornfully. 'Well, I'm sorry but unless I see him right here... And unless I see the mark of the nails and put my finger into those wounds... I will not believe!'

'Thomas?' His name was spoken with love, but Thomas was too angry to notice.

'Thomas...'

Thomas turned. He fell to his knees.

'Go on,' urged Jesus, smiling. 'Put your fingers here. Believe!'

'My Lord...' stuttered Thomas. 'And my God.'

'You believe because you've seen me, Thomas,' said Jesus. 'But even happier are those who will believe without ever having seen me at all.'

# Chapter 12

For a while he came and he went. And when the time came for him to go for ever, they all understood. This was not the end, just the doorway to his Father's house - a house with room for everyone who came. 'Knock,' he'd promised once, 'and the door will be opened.'

'Go through all the earth...' he told the very last crowd, 'and make disciples of every nation.' A gentle wind curled around him.

'I will be with you always,' he promised, with love. 'Even to the end of the world.'

His body had gone, but his spirit remained. Tamar took the hand of a puzzled child. Poor little thing... He didn't understand - yet.

'Don't be upset... In my Father's house are many rooms,' she explained.

'In Capernaum?'

'Yes! In Capernaum, in Jerusalem... in the whole world!' she laughed. 'The Kingdom of God has come, and now he is with us forever.'

*This book is also available as a full-colour
picture storybook illustrated with
over 40 images from the film*

Illustrations courtesy of Cartŵn Cymru and
Icon Entertainment International

Copyright © 2000 SAF Films Ltd and Christmas Films

The right of Sally Humble-Jackson to be identified as the author of
this work has been asserted by her in accordance with the
Copyright, Designs and Patents Act 1988

First published in 2000 by Hodder Children's Books
This edition is for promotional purposes only
Not for resale

ISBN 0340 81761 5

Printed by Guernsey Press

Hodder Children's Books
A division of Hodder Headline Ltd
338 Euston Road
London NW1 3BH